ORANGE BLOSSOM DAYDREAMS

Orange Blossom Daydreams

AKW

WildHaus Publishing

Cover design by AKW
Interior layout and design by AKW
Printed in United States
First Edition: 2024
ISBN: 979-8-218-40756-8

Contents

Part 1   1

Part 2   15

Part 3   28

Part 4   47

Part 1

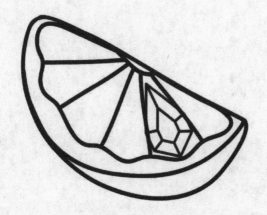

I laughed,
as the sky was turning pink and lavender
and the sun was lifting itself over the mountains
to meet the moon,
and I smashed an empty bottle on your car
to let you know it was over.

Am I going crazy, or coming into my own power?

The loquat tree that stands proud with glossy leaves outside my friend's house on the Eastside could be such a snitch if it wanted to. The things it has seen.

I kissed a man I probably shouldn't have under it. I have walked under it, drunk, belligerent, and laughing. I have eaten its fruit when I am glowing and happy in the summer. Why is every selfie I've taken under it perfect?

The phone calls I've had under it, and the things it's heard. I know it has seen me cry, silent tears and full blown sobbing. It gave me company at 4am, waiting for my Uber to the airport.

Sometimes I wish it would get chopped down because it knows too much about me. But it never will, because the shade is too good and so is the fruit.

And it's the one thing that bore witness to my most intimate, human moments.

Like Venus rising
jasmine intoxicating
tangerines ripening
70 degrees, 9pm
planetary breezes undulating
pacific pheromones
bare feet on velvet loam
sulfuric springs bubbling
under waxing gibbous
Santa Ana winds coaxing
Mercury shifting out of retrograde
the climax of honeysuckle
between the crest and trough of amniotic fluid.

Make me feel this type of way,
and I am yours.

Here is a riddle:

What can be too fat but also too skinny
What can be too lanky but also too short
What can be too promiscuous but also too prude
What can be too dark but also too pale
What can be too ambitious but also too lazy
What can be too loud but too timid
What can be too strong but too weak
All while never being enough.
I am proud to be it but I also resent it.
It can be whore and a mother,
a virgin and a slut,
a lover but just a friend.
What is it?

Answer: a woman

Girl math is:

ending 1 long term-relationship +
losing your mind over 1 situationship +
being ghosted 2 times +
talking to 3 men at once, leading to nothing

= still believing in love

I had already seen your naked body,
bare of tattoos

and I should have known
you couldn't commit.

Forgive me,
because never has anyone been so loud during sex
or gone down on me for so long.
I must have confused lust for love.
But do primates really know the difference?

I have
a thick brain,
angry fists,
a sharp tongue,
and a stubborn heart.

You're not allowed to speak to me in that
tone of voice.

If we need a rat girl summer

to eat bread from the streets
to show ourselves
that we don't need
to eat crumbs from the hands of men,

to navigate dark alleyways
to show ourselves
that we don't need
to be led through broad streets by men,

then so be it.

The night prey became predator:

After a boy's breath sent chills up my spine
because he wanted more than I wanted to give,

After the friend that came to pick me
tried to pull me into his bed,

After I left his house to walk home
and a car began slowly stalking me,

After I hid in the bush at 2am,

I found a loose brick and put my shoulders back,
let my hair down, screaming
fuck you motherfuckers
into the night, canines glistening
and walked myself home.

The feminine urge
to work on an Alaskan crab boat
and toss my phone into the Bering Sea.

Don't shame me,
For I have admitted feelings
that were not reciprocated,
I have mistaken late-night texts
for genuine interest,
I have thought something was something,
when it wasn't anything.

But at least I can say I have loved.

From above
you can see that the clouds
aren't perfectly formed pillows
but a mass of ice crystals and water droplets

and the hell we often call Earth
is a beautifully formed quilt
of forests, farmlands,
mountains, and deserts.

Who would have known
that not everything is as it seems
had we not changed our perspective.

Part 2

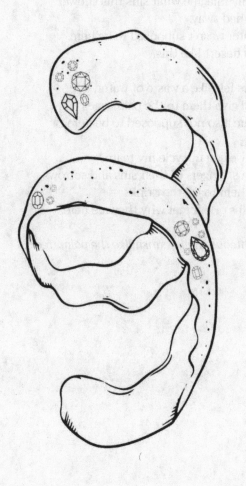

I found myself in child's pose
on the shower floor of a hotel room.
What is more humble than touching one's forehead
where thousands of feet have stood?

I can only imagine what sins this shower
has washed away.
This water wasn't supposed to be here,
not in a desert like this.

My tears felt like a waste of water,
I should give them to the palm trees
that were also not supposed to be here.

Maybe we can upcycle my tears
to clean strangers of their sins and sorrows,
freeze them to ice the drinks
that helps one forget why they are here.

The righteous shall flourish like the palm tree.

I don't need wars or lands in my name,
I don't need a statue of gold in the temple of Venus,
I don't need the Hanging Gardens of Babylon,
I don't need 9 nights of worship,
I just need a text back.

-My self esteem when it is lowest

I have wanted a lot of things for myself in life
to get good grades, to graduate, to be fit,
to travel, to live in a beautiful home.

But sometimes all I have desperately wanted
is to be okay.

I let you give me the death of Prometheus,
my body alone upon a mountain
your words ripping my insides like eagle talons
reliving what you said every day.

If you cannot fathom why
someone might choose to take their own life
or why someone may fill their veins with drugs
or why someone drinks every night
until they black out

you have yet to feel the worst pain of your life.

I would eat pomegranate seeds
from the hands of Hades,
and happily watch all the wildflowers die,
just to hear your voice again.

It cracks the rib cage
without physical force,
It fills the silence in the room
without making a noise,
It consumes me
without being tangible,
Everyone can see it
but no one does anything about it.

-my grief

The candles
The altars
The pyramids
The celebrations
The ceremonies
The flowers
The gods we pray to
The tattoos
The rites
The songs
The dedications
The poems
The photos

All of the things we use to fill the hole
of someone we loved and lost.

To know that a certain moment
may be the last time you hold
someone's physical body in this life;
that is worth all the gold in the world.

If I cut my heart out
while walking over obsidian shards without complaint

If I served you the moon
in a bowl made of pearls from the Tyrrhenian Sea

If I scrubbed out
blood stains from pages of papyrus

that would still not be enough for you.

Sometimes I am so tired
of trying to validate my existence in this world.

I simply want to experience joy
without guilt.

A collapsing dam has the potential
to be incredibly destructive.
Yet it is only nature taking
its original, intended path.
When it's gone,
nature and life comes rushing back in.

Something in your life collapsing
has the potential
to be incredibly destructive.
Yet maybe this is only your life taking
its intended path.

After you've oriented
yourself around the destruction,
are you going to choose to let life back in?

Part 3

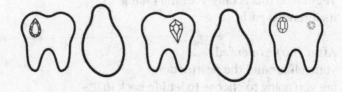

Matilija poppy seeds germinate
when exposed to fire
and it's uncertain
if the heat, the ash, or the smoke
causes the seeds to start growing.

The seeds can sit dormant in the soil
for 20-60 years
until exposed to the element of fire
and then the hillsides explode
in the crepe-paper white blossoms.

And that is how I learned that it's impossible
to separate the pain,
the time,
and sometimes the loss,
from growth.

I scrubbed myself with river stones
to shine for you,
until I felt beautiful.
But then I noticed I was bleeding.

How many times do I need to die
before I am reborn as someone I love?

Did you hate yourself,
or did you hate the version of yourself
that other people made you believe in?

I tripped in the darkness trying to dance,
and when I realized
no one could see the white of my teeth,
I understood that I had led myself in here.

I would bleed myself dry
and set my bones out to bleach in Death Valley
to not become you.

You will have to say no thousands of times
to other people

until you are able to say yes
to yourself.

I want to burn it all down.

I set the house on fire while I was still inside
and now I'm trying to figure out
how to leave.

I do not know what is going to happen.

But I do know
even the deepest point of the ocean
has a bottom,
and the driest desert
receives rain.

Why did you do that?
Why would you say that?
Why did you hurt me?
Why can't you just apologize?
What did you think that was okay?
Why did you...

Why did I give you the keys to hurt me?

Helping someone
who doesn't want to help themselves
is trying to catch a falling sun from the sky,
and wondering why your hands are scorched.

If I stayed,
I would have had roses
thrown at my feet for eternity.

But I would have had
to walk over thorns
to do what I want.

Remember: your power is that you know you can
wear the heads of men as a necklace
and topple empires

but you choose not to.

Broken shards of glass that you call trash
they too can become smooth
in the right conditions.

-The people that find sea glass beautiful

We are taught to view the glass half full,
rather than half empty.
I think that lesson is easy enough to understand.

But how about the glass
filled to the brim, threatening to spill over?

We should also be taught
how to accept an overflowing glass
from loving hands.

But what about the glass
that is less than a quarter full?

We should also be taught
to walk away
when someone is trying to convince us
that it is half full.

When I lose faith in humanity
I go to sit somewhere
and I people watch, observing and wondering

Who else is fighting a silent battle,
trying to hold it together in public?

until I feel tears in my eyes
and the urge to embrace everyone.

My dad taught me
how to drive a boat on Father's Day
and it probably felt like
when he taught me how to ride a bike,
except this time we had beers in hand and I was 26.

There was nothing we were worried about,
we didn't speak of the pain and the loss,
and it was a perfect afternoon on the lake.
Why can't it always be like this?

But I realized
instead of wasting my time
wishing for the impossible

I must experience these moments
with every ounce of my presence
and save it perfectly in my memory,
so I *can* experience it whenever I would like.

The Sahara desert becomes green
every 21,000 years
and I decorate my teeth with gems
Don't you dare tell me
it's not a miracle to exist here and now.

Part 4

If plants do best
when the dead unproductive parts
are trimmed away
why can't you do the same?

Brown leaves sat heavily upon my branches
threatening to rot away the healthy parts
so I gave myself an early spring.

Plants aren't supposed to feel pain
but I think I felt something
when I stripped away the brown leaves
and when I bloomed like the flowers
tattooed on my body.

My Roman Empire
is that when I'm outside and alone,
suddenly I don't feel like the crazy one.

We played "Mother May I"
always taking 1 step forward and 3 steps back
until I didn't want to protect your feelings anymore
and I chose to walk under the jacaranda trees alone.

Since I left, you should know:

I learned how to make an ofrenda
from cempasúchils
I crossed the Strait of Gibraltar by ferry
and made it through Shibuya crossing
I danced in Mama Rumba
and I picked Valencian oranges from the tree.

If I can still feel gratitude
from the first sip of hot coffee in the early morning
I know that not all is lost.

https://www.youtube.com/watch?v=34PJMUVHZGw

how I began to heal
and how I knew I wasn't alone

(Billie Eilish - Happier Than Ever, Live
Life is Beautiful Festival 2021)

It cracks the rib cage
without physical force
It fills the silence in the room
without making a noise
It consumes me
and I let it
Everyone can see it,
and I share it.

-my hope

If you find someone who unpacks your pain
like they would help you unpack your suitcase
after a long trip

Treating all the things
you don't want someone else to see;
your mismatched socks,
coffee stained T-shirt,
a pair of worn underwear.

And treating them like
your favorite Levi's that hug your ass
and pretty lingerie.
Folding, separating,
washing, removing stains,
and mending tears.
Then you might be able to stay awhile.

(And if they don't even offer to lift the suitcase
up the stairs, what is the point?)

Life is going to be hard for you
if you can remember your entire childhood
from smelling an old T-shirt packed away in a box.

If you can describe what summer tastes like
and you can feel someone's emotions
without any words.

If you listen to that one song on repeat
for 7 days straight and it still hits.

If you feel like you're wilting
under grocery store lighting
and you feel like you're going to die in a crowd.

If reading an old text
can bring you to your knees
and tears form in your eyes
from the scent of blown-out birthday cake candles.

Life is going to be hard for you,
but you're going to experience it so deeply.

I can be tricked
into thinking that cars on the highway
are the murmur of the ocean

I could believe
with squinted eyes, that the distant city lights
are constellations

For a moment
I thought the lit-up Shell gas station sign
was a full moon

But never again will I allow someone to convince me
that I am undeserving of love.

Who I am
Because I am my uncle's prison time
My mother's rage and her sunflowers
My grandmother's poultry factory wage
and her last pack of cigarettes
My brother's jacket pockets
filled with candy wrappers
My grandpa's shotgun for scaring off coyotes
My uncle's tangelo farm
My brother's full ride scholarship
My dad's Costco box wine
and the *"Don't blame me, I voted for Trump"*
sticker on the side of his Silverado

So who am I
without my orange blossom daydreams?

For the first time in years
I caught myself smiling for no reason

and it brought tears to my eyes
because I didn't want to punch myself in the face

and for the first time in years
I knew I was going to be okay.

Why Orange Blossom Daydream?

My grandparents raised my mother in an area surrounded by orange trees and citrus farms. The land here has a perfect perfume of orange blossoms during the right time of the year. My mother raised me in a town not so far from here, and I too had the privilege of growing up surrounded by orange trees and their perfume.

My uncle owns and operates a tangelo farm in the San Joaquin Valley. When I was a child, this was my first exposure to farming and what it looked like to make a living from the land. My uncle depended on nature to make a living and provide for his family. To me, this was beautiful, but I also saw how incredibly challenging this way of life could be.

Orange blossoms have existed through the entirety of my adolescence and adulthood. It is my favorite scent, and smelling it always draws me to my past, and it also serves as a reminder to reconnect with the natural environment around me. The scent of orange blossoms represents hope, love, growth, and the sweetness of life despite all of its ugliness.

Even in my darkest times, the scent can still remind me of this. In my darkest times, I dream of the good feelings that the smell of orange blossoms bring me.

Finally, I have finished writing this collection of poems in Valencia, Spain. It is a city known for the abundance orange trees that line the streets and plazas, and the intoxicating scent of orange blossoms during spring.

Thank you for reading and your support.

-AKW

Printed in the USA
CPSIA information can be obtained
at www.ICGtesting.com
LVHW030822210724
786027LV00007B/456

9 798218 407568